2/11

D1124646

Country Music Stars

MIRANDA LAMBERT

By Aife Franke

Gareth Stevens
Publishing

Please visit our Web site, www.garethstevens.com. For a free color catalog of all our high-quality books, call toll free 1-800-542-2595 or fax 1-877-542-2596.

Library of Congress Cataloging-in-Publication Data

Franke, Aife.
  Miranda Lambert / Aife Franke.
     p. cm. — (Country music stars)
  Includes index.
  ISBN 978-1-4339-3936-5 (pbk.)
  ISBN 978-1-4339-3937-2 (6-pack.)
  ISBN 978-1-4339-3935-8 (library binding)
  1. Lambert, Miranda, 1983—Juvenile literature. 2. Country musicians—United States—Biography—Juvenile literature. I. Title.
  ML3930.L145F73 2011
  782.421642092—dc22
  [B]
                                        2010002249

First Edition

Published in 2011 by
Gareth Stevens Publishing
111 East 14th Street, Suite 349
New York, NY 10003

Copyright © 2011 Gareth Stevens Publishing

Designer: Haley W. Harasymiw
Editor: Therese Shea

Photo credits: Cover background Shutterstock.com; cover (Miranda Lambert), pp. 1, 7, 11 Rick Diamond/Getty Images; pp. 5, 17, 19, 27, 29 Ethan Miller/Getty Images; pp. 9, 13 Kevin Winter/Getty Images; p. 15 Frederick Breedon/Getty Images; pp. 21, 23 John Russell/WireImage; p. 25 Richard Carson/WireImage.

Printed in the United States of America

CPSIA compliance information: Batch #CS10GS: For further information contact Gareth Stevens, New York, New York at 1-800-542-2595.

CONTENTS

MEET MIRANDA

Miranda Lambert is known for her fearless country music. She is not afraid to be herself.

Miranda Lambert was born on November 10, 1983. She grew up in Lindale, Texas.

Miranda's parents were detectives. Her father also played the guitar. He often invited people to their house to listen to music.

9

YOUNG SINGER

When Miranda was 10, she saw a Garth Brooks concert. She told her father she wanted to be a singer.

Garth Brooks

Miranda's father gave her a guitar when she was 14 years old. However, Miranda did not want to learn to play.

13

Miranda entered many singing contests. She did not like some of the songs she was asked to sing.

15

LEARNING THE GUITAR

Miranda asked her father to teach her to play the guitar. She wanted to write her own music.

17

When she was 17, Miranda formed a band called Texas Pride. They often played at a famous ballroom.

19

THE BIG BREAK

In 2001, Miranda's father recorded her music. Miranda played her music for radio stations. She finished high school early.

21

Miranda's family traveled around Texas. She played her music in many places. In 2003, she tried out for a TV show called *Nashville Star*.

23

A NASHVILLE STAR

Nashville Star was a contest for country music singers. Miranda won third place. A record company asked her to make music. She said yes!

25

Miranda's first album was number one on the country music charts. Her next two albums were named Album of the Year!

SHE MEANS IT

Miranda says she means every word she sings. She writes most of her own songs. Miranda's fans love her!

TIMELINE

1983   Miranda is born November 10 in Lindale, Texas.

1993   Miranda sees a Garth Brooks concert.

1997   Miranda gets a guitar as a gift from her father.

2000   Miranda forms a band.

2003   Miranda sings on the TV show *Nashville Star*.

2005   Miranda's first album comes out.

FOR MORE INFORMATION

Books:

Handyside, Chris. *Country*. Chicago, IL: Heinemann
Library, 2006.

Riggs, Kate. *Country Music*. Mankato, MN: Creative
Education, 2008.

Web Sites:

CMT.com: Miranda Lambert
www.cmt.com/artists/az/lambert_miranda/artist.jhtml

Miranda Lambert Official Site
www.mirandalambert.com

Nashville Star
www.nashvillestar.com

GLOSSARY

ballroom: a large room used for dances

concert: a public music event

contest: a test of skills among people, usually for a prize

detective: one who works to uncover lawbreaking or other information

record: to make a copy of sounds

record company: a business that produces and sells music

INDEX